I KNOW WELL THE FACE OF DESPAIR

I KNOW WELL THE FACE OF DESPAIR

Hatem Al Shahri

Translated from Arabic by

Jinane Khashouf & Abdulrahman Jones

Edited by Helen Wing

NOMAD PUBLISHING

I KNOW WELL THE FACE OF DESPAIR

Hatem Al Shahri

This book was translated as part of the Tarjim Initiative
مبادرة
ترجم
Tarjim Initiative

Published by Nomad Publishing in 2023
Email: info@nomad-publishing.com
www.nomad-publishing.com

ISBN 9781914325472

The Publishers would like
to thank the Harf Literary Agency

Contents

Foreword

When Nomad told me they were going to publish a range of contemporary Saudi Arabian poetry collections, I was very excited. It would be a huge privilege to look through the window of poetry at a world with which so few Western non-Arabic speaking readers are familiar. I had little doubt that I would find the poetry produced in the context of the geography, history and culture of Saudi Arabia to be fascinating, unique and, very possibly, opaque to me. And I was also concerned that in a region such as the Gulf, so often plagued by the received stereotypical assumptions of outsiders, the voices of its poets should not be belied or misunderstood, especially if translation into another tongue threatened to bring with it contentions of meaning and lexical or ideological impositions.

I believe this collection of poets provides a fascinating showcase for themes both relevant and necessary for a greater understanding of Saudi Arabian culture. I discovered in it poetry of immense diversity in both form and theme: poetry about identity, isolation and relationships with family and friends, surreal poetry about one's relationship with the object world and with a metamorphic natural world, poetry about Bedouin culture and about the traditions of Arabic poetry and Arabic history and Islam, poetry about poverty, poetry steeped in myth and storytelling.

In *Emptiness in a Long Line*, **Mohammed Kheder** warns us to stay true to ourselves in the face of the onslaught of the modern, the constant battering by the news and the awareness that time is a succession of moments and feelings falling constantly out of our reach. In *Development*, he shows us how the photograph creates the myths of our existence, making us conscious of how we see. For him, photos create a 'unique connection with things we see for the first time /

and how they transform into icons as wide as we can see.' In his love poetry, in *Return my Head to its Normal Position*, he documents in minute detail the anticipation of love, its ecstasy and the way the world transforms for the lovers and love's eventual disintegration.

In *A Life as Big as a Packet of Cigarettes*, **Al Hussain Moafa** protests, with a rare and gorgeous lyricism, the injustices of poverty and of a powerless, restricted life. In stark hopelessness he begs to reclaim some beauty in his life, 'Give me back my banned books. / I will return your chants and anthems. / Who among you cast this night upon me? / Lift me from the depths of darkness, / withdraw your slithering tongues, / like the threads of cassette tapes. / Give me back the words I wrote, / release me from this cell as wide / as a packet of cigarettes.'

In **Shtiwi Al Githi's** *A Tale of Ancient Whiteness* Western audiences have a fascinating glimpse of the subtlety and depth of a nomadic imagination, of the desert mind, forged in deep experience of topography, philosophy and knowledge of the

Quran and of the ancient traditions of Arabic poetry.

In *The Clouds that Pass*, **Atheer Al Nashmi** also mines the history of Arabic culture viewing it through a contemporary lens with often absurd and comic intent. His aim is to throw a light on the delusions we live by and the contradictions we inhabit.

And in stark contrast, **Hatem Al Shahri** in *I Know Well the Face of Despair*, looks despair in the face in his elegy and lament for language. His is a poetry of isolation and despair. And it is language itself that restricts the poet, shutting him out of a sense of joy or access to the sublime. And finally, in **Mohammed Ibrahim Yacoub**'s *A Place of Forgetfulness*, we encounter spiritual poetry in the tradition of the mystic, of Sufism. Here the poet yearns for the sublime in both divine and human love, plotting his exile on Earth as a preternatural expulsion from Eden, from grace, in the fall of Adam, 'I recognize every absence by its name. / I am exiled in loss, like Adam.' In this deeply religious poetry, poetry itself becomes an act of worship where the poet seeks the hidden depths of the soul, convinced that this world is but a shadow of true life, 'I am other than myself, my words not all I convey, / my desires not all I fulfil on life's journey every day.' His poems are often declamatory acts of prayer in praise of love, both divine and human, as he exhorts us to, 'Like the howling wolf mocking every loss, / elevate your spirit, to the sky's pure gloss!' His poetry reverberates with the tradition of a thousand years of mystical Arabic poetry as he protests our restriction to our fleshly mortal selves and begs us to to, 'Shatter the cursed clay and find a brighter way!'

Again and again, through these poets, the reader is given an impression of the immensity of space in both the desert and the sky, the great expanses of the geography of Saudi Arabia that free the humble human soul into a sense of belonging and indubitable emotional attachment to the place that is Saudi Arabia. Indeed, I have come to understand, I feel, a little of the spiritual pull that Makkah exerts in the world of Islam in these gentle, lyrical portrayals of place.

The emotional complexity and intellectual sophistication of contemporary Saudi Arabian poetry offers a huge variety of poetic forms, including couplets, prose poems, fragmentary free verse and lyrical storytelling. The forms of Arabic poetry, so challenging to attempt to render in English, also serve an abundance of tonal variety for poets who speak with a tender humour, for those who struggle to express feelings of alienation or failure, and for those who inhabit the meta-literary realms of their ancient poetic tradition.

Most striking for me in each and every one though, is the plangent honesty of the poetic voices in this collection, which leads me to the conviction that the task of poetry, the adding of something new and beautiful to the world, is indeed achieved in this impressive, new collection of Saudi Arabian poetry in English.

To my friend

Azrael

Running away from the Disaster of Birth

Dr. Moussa Rahim Abbas

In my collaboration on Hatem Al Shahri's 'I Know Well the Face of Despair', I could not help but recall the Romanian-born French thinker and writer, Emil Cioran (1911-1995), for he was our source of inspiration for confessions and curses as he celebrated the everyday and the ordinary by addressing questions with broad answers about life, death, beginning, birth, without any restraint, to the point of saying, 'The only books that deserve to be written are those whose authors do not think of their readers.' And, so it is with Hatem Al Shahri, whose writings are snapshots that mock existence and all that does not belong to the truth, that is mere speculation.

And I agree with Cioran: although we are light years away from poetry, we still need to be part of the lyric, of an art that does not run towards death, but rather flees from the disaster of birth, as Cioran puts it; and this makes of Al Shahri a scarecrow that scares away hopes and desires. He worries about the shape of his soul and dreams of clothing the streets with humanity again, wrapping himself in the patience to do so. He still drags along his childhood grief, which is the launch pad to his cemetery. And no matter how he expresses himself in fresh and transparent language, he knows that his voice dies at his own hands, letter by letter, leaving only three letters (M, T, W). But do we have to believe what he says? Has he really announced his defeat in the battle of life? I personally don't trust poets: from their despair comes life, like a phoenix flying from North to South.

Riyadh

15th of December, 2020

Depression is my Profession

Foreword to the Book,

"I Know Well the Face of Despair" by Hatem Al Shahr

By: Dr. Muhammad Jamal Tahan

I know the face of despair very well, which means that hope is near because the enemy is known. Do you think that Hatem Al-Shahri hides the paths that life may offer us with his words? It seems that this is not the case, as dedicating this book to his friend Azrael is a sign of how pessimistic he is about this life, and how little hope he has for the next. And amongst the problems of today, he cites the difficulty of finding a loyal friend. His short verses reflect the writer's desires and lost dreams in this world, where he is wrapped in loneliness, an image of the pain caused by the loss of his friends. His disappointment begins at birth: all around the dead are scattered at the crossroads between life and death. He stands there lonely as a scarecrow striking terror into hope and desire. His soul seeks to resolve contradiction, seeks balance, seeks to break down barriers. How, then, can he find happiness among lyrical verses? Hatem travels the lyrical road with his pockets full of clouds, and all he can see at the end of the road is death. He knows the face of despair all too well, for it brings with it all the evils of the world, including the permanence of loss and bad luck.

He has no time for sadness; he uses his words to throw sorrow out of the window of love. Hatem faces human wolves, is afraid, resists, suffers pain, then falls in love with himself and hurls himself at life using words as his shield. But Hatem does not ask himself, 'What comes next?' So, he enters the prime of life, sailing in sadness until he gets drunk on it. When Autumn knocks at his door, his vision becomes clearer, broader as this is when we reach supreme love, supreme wonder, supreme joy, but also extreme sadness. And so, as we become accustomed to an array of emotions felt all at the same time, we also become prone to depression.

Does he have time for melancholy? If you ever manage to master boredom, the days will quickly go by as your mental state changes from one to another before being exposed to the real world. In this way, you'll be able to protect yourself from depression, from your recurring attempts to drown in life. Hatem does not deny himself melancholy: he refers to the gaping hole in memory where joy, sadness and friends seep in. Now, he who identifies himself with others, absorbs every emotion until he reaches a dreadful satiety, becoming drunk with depression. At its peak he reaches a melancholic ecstasy that shatters the tranquillity of his soul. When you are dominated by depression, you go through rage. But when you overcome your moods and accept feeling overwhelmed, you grow up. And at that moment, you feel like a king, a king who clings to his throne like a child who does not want to share his toys. And only then will you not suffer boredom! There's no time for melancholy, Hatem! We are too busy trying not to drown from life's struggles. Only when you change your habits will you see whether there is room for melancholy.

Love the innocence in your texts, the innocence that is still discovering what experience has not yet revealed! Love this, for it will not wither no matter how much time goes by!

From your writing will come the Spring and an end to melancholy. AAnd the truth, O Hatem, is that writing is the revelation of depression.

In the Next Life

In my next life God will
grant me
beautiful handwriting.
No one will think I cast spells
or create talismans.

In my next life I hope
I never have to
queue again.
I've done more than
my fair share in this one.

In my next life I will
be loan-free.

In my next life God will
reimburse me for every book
my friends stole under the pretext
of borrowing, and I'll be grateful
for pens that don't stain my clothes.

In my next life God will
reveal to me and only me
the secret of the best seller,
and maybe, just maybe, I will
own a kiosk selling love and warmth.

And I will hold the biggest feast
honouring my everlasting love for novels.

IN THE NEXT LIFE

There has to be a next life
where I am blessed
with friends, real friends
in sorrow as in joy.

I do not doubt there will be
a next life for me...

Dear Death, Have a Safe Trip!

You who defend Life, have you ever been able
to anticipate the hardships of life's journey?
Have you ever undone
the traps set by bad omens?

Me? I'm oblivious to despair's arrows
raining down from the mountain of archers…
Enclosed in trenches of good faith, I barely
notice the desolate mines laid by my enemy.

Enchanted by Life's dazzling glory therefore
I say, 'Dear Death, Have a safe trip!'

Room Zero

Cut down by words and abominable expectations,
Shot down by the bullets of criticism, each
expressed with 'malicious intent.'

Diagnosed with the fourth-degree burns
of mankind's deceit, I lie traumatized, bleeding, dying,
hiding my contemptible, naked face:
this total emotional breakdown, has beaten me
into silence.

You may find me at the Hospital of the Beloved,
The Intensive Care Unit of idiom and phrase,
the sole patient in Room Zero.

Luxury Incentive

(for Layla and her neighbour)

I practice waiting for death and life...

Have you thought about suicide?

No, but when I think about life, suicide would be a start...

I always think about my courage as being alive until now…

I have the herd instinct to survive.

I want to take revenge and travel to Hades...

I don't have the luxury of incentives.

I want to take the train, but I'll miss the trip.

What Will They Call Me?

Despite the hard life I've had
I'll go into the fire when it's over.
(When the clouds become weary and sink down,
no one recognises them. They call it fog!!!)
And when I get tired, what will they call me?

Loneliness

Tears after sadness are replaced by another
sensation. I close my eyes, but no tears fall...
My friends let go of my hand...I leave the bridge,
the cities collapse, there is no more family.
I, the bearer of unity, descend into a valley
of isolation and self-centeredness...
I am the discoverer of individuality, the first
to own it. I become more individual, solitary.
I used to know the days by the calendar,
now I know them by the length of my beard.
The more friends abandoned me, the worse I became.
I dread the day when I can no longer write.
If I were looking for gold, I could find it; but I'm looking

for the most precious thing in the world: a friend.

There are no friends anymore, not even in hardship.

There is so little time… it's as if the days are forbidden

to bring us together.

If you had not Come into this World

Pure happiness exists in nothingness, in non-existence. Your arrival in this world is really a new disappointment, a sharp knife, a stab in the back – (Don't look for the knife: the scar tells all the story)

There is no one here to Pity us

Poor you, if you think that the dead are only in the cemeteries...

Or perhaps you think they are in literary clubs, in concerts,
and in the most important neighbourhoods?

Oh, but their names don't appear on the obituary page...

We are here, the dead (and there is no one here to pity us).

Alone as a Scarecrow

The cord of hope was not left behind.

It's around my neck...

I thought lying was only its thread

but I also find hope.

I'm alone as a scarecrow,

scared and hopeless,

and wishing, thinking,

... and the birds...

What is My Soul Like?

I read this sentence.

I remember my father saying

if you want to look into someone's soul,

you must ask them to show you their dreams.

I went back to my dream list and found it.

A funeral cortege at night with a fancy dress party

in the cemetery....

Loading a gun and shooting it in the open air....

The dream of printing a letter of thanks

for the memorial

at the beginning of the city…

I would like to set up a charitable alliance
for all the contributors in the tents
and free them from their families...

I dream of finding a balance between sugar and salt
and breaking the barrier between them...

My dream is to be an official sponsor of the first
sex change operation in the tribe,
of the first sex-change operation
in the salt tribe.

And to produce salt now...I dream of
bringing back the clothes that you walk in
down the street, of dressing you in humanity.

These are some of my dreams,
So, what is my soul like?

Bound to Mischief

Your presence in this life is a 'slight error'.
Your ship is drifting away from the shore,

It's sinking... but expectation simmers
and the winds rise up to change my fate...

The purchase of a suit of patience in my size,
and the second day begins.

It's all up to you...
Just one day...

Just one day and my dream will come true.
I'll know as soon as your ship arrives!

What are you Hiding in your Pocket?

I put my hand in my pocket
and passers-by ask me:
'What are you hiding
in your pocket?'

'I'm hiding six misfortunes,
ten disappointments,
thirteen bottles of pain.
I'm hiding my childhood dreams.'

The adults look disgusted.
I hide my empty hand.
And in the other
I have nothing.

Misery Blooms

The smell of misery wafts out from my house,
You can smell it from four miles away.

Night calamities, seven sudden calamities...
I fell into the well...
No car saved me, and I have no brothers.

There's a gang of pains, like nations.
I speak nine languages, the last one is smiling…
in a splint, bleeding...

I speak the language of charity (I'm fine!), ...
also, the language of laughter (Hahaha!) ...
I speak the language of tears:
the rain in my eyes, not the sky.

Pet

Curing my sadness since I was a child...

When travelling, it was written on the ticket,

'No pets allowed'.

Always prevented from coming with us,

was my pain a pet?

The City of False Hope

I am a balcony overlooking a cemetery...

I'm a graveyard of dreams, I catch birds...

Death in Valley Park.

Every day I share out the dreams,

until the graves are filled...

I have a scalpel and a band-aid.

I make cuts.

The dreams arrive in droves behind me,

and I fix them up with plasters.

'Will I walk lame like this forever
or will I die?' they seem to say.

'I don't remember a dream
that went on to the end.
They tell me to be strong
but until when?'

'Until Judgment Day when you
will be melted under the rays
of disappointment, destroyed
in the fire of calamity...
a failed iron project, melted at Anaconda...

Maybe one day I will be a map,
guidelines for the city of Amani…'

Death in the Alphabet

There were twenty-eight in my drawer.

Literally use them as needed.

Every day one of them dies...

And suddenly, a tribe of letters died.

I only see four left:

Mawt*.

*Death

One Victory

It's okay to lose. In some cases
It might be comforting.

I invited her home; we went to the basement.
There, I saw my daily losses.

She saw a sign hanging on the door:
'It's okay to win in some cases.'

Life: one big loss, one victory.

Tree of Zaqqoum

If God created me as a tree, I would be zaqqoum;

but he made me a man.

I'm looking for 'opportunity' to knock on my door.

Everything but opportunity knocks on my door:

Debts

Neighbours

Torrents

Misfortunes...

What about opportunity?

Opportunity is blind to my door...

Wish Enchanter

I hate the mirror.

It almost ruined my voice.

I once saw a store that sold friends....

I wish I were a friend so someone would buy me....

I wouldn't want to take me...

I hang my future on a wishing pin.

I come back in the afternoon...

I find my future killing me.

Silver Spoon

My life is a subway, not a train from Vienna.
I have an international license at the crossroads.
I marvel at those who are born with a golden spoon
in their mouths.
I know the gold, but I don't know the spoon.

Cups Upside Down

I sing alone, for the lost, for the wind, for wounded time...

I pour my voice into inverted cups.

I howl to myself; I sing by myself.

Theatre of life...

Since I became famous, no one comes to see me.

I am not dreaming, but singing to a mirage....

I lose my voice in the anguished pit of life...

I want to buy ears to listen to myself;

Loving the soundtrack...

I desire the storm and intensity of the audience;

but I do not like the neighbourhood crowd.

Hadily will not stand up for just anyone,

and this place full of emptiness and noise

makes for silence.

Once the room is full, I'll cut out my throat,

throw it away for the stray dogs to eat

and what's left will be hoarse.

Drowning on Land

I was drowning on dry land....

‘He sank and it was over.

We were able to help him;

It seemed somehow

he would make it through.’

I Know Well the Face of Despair

From the window of patience, despair walks to the door.

I've become addicted to observing it....

He brings his brothers with him, and does not come alone.

I protect myself with patience; but courage prevails.

I hoped to die alone...

His brothers call me every night.

I will not die alone, for I know

The face of despair brings good luck…

Defeated

I've been defeated all my life.

...I am a shadow striker,

an actor in the background,

… an emergency landing...

I never really prayed...

…life sucked me in.

'I don't want anyone to feel sorry for me.

But it's clear to everyone: I am defeated.'

I Miss Being a Rose

I cried while at the movies.
I went with my loneliness:
the empty seat broke my heart.

Alone, I came as Da'ad Haddad.

My stem bent down to the ground...
I missed being a rose
but I was OK being a cactus.

When did it turn off?

I want to answer; but the question

came too late.

A Very Sad Victory

You were a disaster of hope,
a calamity of good tidings.

We were quietly close...but now
you are far away and lonely.

What your hands have ruined,
drugs won't fix.

I defeated you, and sadly
this was a very sad victory!

Like a Rose

There is a myth that says that aloe vera

was the 'rose' of the past.

But she was abused so many times

that she decided to protect herself.

And to do so, she grew wings, not fangs.

I'm like a rose.

I don't cry, but I am falling…

Here and There

When a trainer throws in the towel in the boxing ring,

the match is over, and this is a sign of surrender.

I want to throw my towel into the ring of life.

I have done, but the match is still being played.

It seems that life loves me very much

And I obligingly live, under life arrest.

Damn universe. I wish I were a mill.

But I'm a woman with breasts full of milk.

I hope I'm a hard word to swallow.

I used to wish I was a tree, but I gave up.

And what about giving up and the damage it causes?

Don't I have enough time to change, delete and add wishes?

Life is long to write a long list of wishes.

I once sat with death as the elevator closed in on me.

Happy, for I was finally going to receive my order.

But alas, the 'saviours' arrived.

They cut my beautiful dream short and I was stuck here.

And how hard is the word 'here' when you want to be 'there.'

How many times I was lucky enough to see Azrael from afar;

but every time I did, I heard the whisper that 'not yet'.

My friend, Azrael, I don't want to work here anymore.

I don't want to do any more overtime.

I don't want to be the milk in a cow's udder

Nor the dirt in the cloth,

The only thing important to me is to be 'there'.

Plastic Wings

Won't these wings hurt me?

Fly with them. You'll become stronger.

I wish I could, but they are made of plastic!

When do you Cry?

She asked me: when do you cry?
And I said who said I cry?

I only cry in moments of joy, sorrow and
before going to sleep.
Does it count to cry when watching movies?
Or when watching goals, or in competitions?

It's a very strange question, as I rarely cry.
I have cried very little in life, and I only remember crying
when I listening to music, see paintings or
when I read poetry,
when reading poetry…

I cry when the night falls and the dawn breaks...

I cry on vacations, and in the middle of work,

when coming up to the vacations...

I cry at weddings, at cemeteries,

also, in gardens,

because of successes,

because of defeats.

Peace makes me cry, travels too.

I cry when I'm in bed, when I look in the mirror,

in airports, museums and mosques....

in mosques…

When I walk into gift stores,

when I receive a bouquet of roses.

So, when you ask me: When do you cry?

When I stop crying, I cry…

My Last Attempt

This is my last attempt, if I try at all.
I failed and set my poem on fire.
I burned dreams, desires and premonitions.
Now I will worship God and not believe in hope.
This is my last attempt.

I have a little pouch in which I put my big dreams
And I have a sledgehammer to smash
all the dreams that I accumulate.
My bones are shattered
just like my dreams were shattered...

I had a weapon I prepared for my enemies
and it exploded in my hand: I got a shiver
as a token of the vengeance between us.

I could have sworn this was my last attempt.
I'll kill my butterflies and I'll kill my dog,
and leave food for them to enjoy in heaven.

If the next one is the same as the one
who just left, this will definitely be my last try.

My Size is Small

What do you say to someone who is getting
ready to leave you?
I may not be the size of your dreams.

Sadly, I would understand.
My problem is size.

All my life my habits have been very narrow,
as have my sizes.
I can't find a shirt that fits me for my size,
nor pants, nor shoes nor keffiyeh.

But happiness I'm finding has no size. She made herself tight clothes.

The happiness I find is designed for people younger than me.

As for happiness on a large scale, it has not yet been created.

And I don't know if I've seen it, or whether it even exists.

Who knows of a store that sells the size of happiness?

I'm still looking…